the power of

Meditation

a guide for beginners

Sister Jayanti

BRAHMA KUMARIS

BKIS

The Power of Meditation
A Guide for Beginners

Sister Jayanti

Print: ISBN 978-1-886872-59-2
Kindle: 978-1-886872-71-4
EPub: 978-1-886872-72-1

First edition: first published in 2015
Copyright © 2014 Brahma Kumaris Information Services Ltd.,
Publications Division, London

Published by Brahma Kumaris Information Services Ltd. in
Association with Brahma Kumaris World Spiritual University (UK)
registered Charity No. 269971

Global Co-operation House,
65 Pound Lane,
London NW10, 2HH UK

other books by

Sister Jayanti

Awaken Your Inner Wisdom

Dreams & Reality

God's Healing Power

Practical Meditation

Spirituality in Daily Life

The Art of Thinking

Contents

How to use this book

This is the only book you'll need to begin meditating. It can be used by the beginner thanks to its step-by-step approach; it can also bring clarity and newness to those who have already been practising meditation for some time. The book comprises a quick course of lessons in Raja Yoga meditation that allows you to dip your toe into the water and find out how good meditation can make you feel, and how it can improve your every interaction with others.

You don't need to subscribe to a religion to sample and gain benefits from this form of meditation – it is there for people of all faiths and none, and it is easy to follow whatever your age or background.

The book explains how to meditate in easy-to-follow terms and it is simple to put the ideas into practice – you don't need to learn complicated postures or breathing techniques, or buy expensive props. All you need is a comfortable chair, a little quiet time and the inclination to look inside yourself and reflect honestly on what you see.

The very practical exercises in each chapter will help you to stop, look inside yourself and find that you are effortlessly practising meditation – this introductory guide shows that meditation really can be that easy and that rewarding.

The benefits of meditation

Meditation is a means of looking inside ourselves, at our thoughts and feelings, seeing what is happening and then transforming the quality of our thinking so that it becomes elevated. The effect of this often lasts longer than the 20 or 30 minutes of a meditation session. With practice, our consciousness will remain elevated throughout the day. This then impacts on our energy levels and all our relationships; not just with ourselves but also with others. When we connect with the spirit in each other – the beings of light that we truly are – respectful relationships develop with all those around us.

When I give talks about meditation I look around the audience and see people from so many different backgrounds... this tells me that there is something universal that draws people to meditation – the same motivation that brought you to this book perhaps. One factor is that we are all souls, irrespective of our supposed differences, usually based on physical qualities, such as our gender, age or race. A second factor is that we all share the same parent, the Supreme Soul, a being of light, and whether we know it or not, we all wish at some level to reconnect with that source of light, power and love.

You might not have had any visions of light or ecstatic experiences – that is quite OK because such experiences are not the purpose of meditation. The purpose of meditation is to communicate... to move our thoughts in the direction of God so that we can connect with and receive from God the divine qualities that already exist deep inside ourselves, but which we have lost as we have journeyed through life. Then all the dust we have gathered along the way, which has concealed and clogged up our innate qualities, will be washed away so that our innate highest attributes can emerge.

So if that is the aim of meditation – to connect with God – what are the results of renewing this connection? The result is that we discover and are able to put to use our many inner powers: the power of love, the power of peace, the power of purity, the power of truth and the power of happiness. Once you have discovered all these inner virtues, you will have such incredible inner power that nothing outside can touch you. Everyday life continues, life events take you up one moment and down the next, but despite this, when you are in touch with your inner powers you remain calm and peaceful and know what to say, what to do and how to help. This is the true power of meditation – and this book shows you how to discover it.

The health benefits

Meditation is an ancient tradition that developed in India thousands of years ago as a means of developing spiritual awareness through self-discipline and mental focusing techniques. In the 20th century, medical practitioners began to study the effects of meditation on the body and mind. Many have focused on the ability of meditative techniques to combat stress, which is a contributing factor in so many diseases that have burgeoned in the modern era, from heart complaints to depression. Many studies since the 1950s, for example, have shown how meditation causes the heart and respiratory rates to slow, blood pressure to lower, and electrical activity in the skin to reduce. Some studies have even suggested that meditation is more effective in achieving this relaxation response than other techniques routinely recommended by doctors to combat stress disorders, including progressive relaxation exercises, biofeedback and simple sitting in silence with eyes closed. Meditators studied by other researchers have shown increased blood flow to the brain, and an increased ability to recover quickly from the impact of stress.

In a 2010 study lead by Professor Jim Lagopoulos of Sydney University, Australia and researchers from the Norwegian University of Science and Technology (NTNU), meditators were asked to meditate wearing equipment that picked up electrical changes in the brain. The researchers found that when the meditators entered a state of inner silence, their brainwaves changed, with increased alpha-wave activity in the posterior part of the brain, associated with wakeful rest. So as we begin to meditate, the speed of thoughts slows down and we pass from the regular goal-orientated beta state of consciousness of everyday life into the alpha state. Within this alpha state there is a doorway into spirituality. When we open this door we begin to access the deeper part of consciousness. When the experienced meditators in the study continued to meditate, they went on to experience a sense of communion, and theta waves were observed in the front and top of the brain, parts of the brain linked with the limbic system, the centre of emotion and mood. In this state the speed of thoughts is much, much slower. In the theta state we are able to experience personal insight, creativity, moments of realisation and a deep state of understanding. There is another state of consciousness described by scientists – the delta state. In the delta state brainwaves are even slower. When we enter this state, we experience great empathy and a sense of connectedness with the whole family of the globe. We are also able to connect with our own deep intuition and innermost emotions. The state between the theta state of realisation and creativity and the delta state of connection is often described as a place where self-healing takes place.

In Raja Yoga we would say that the alpha state is when you are thinking in a positive way and making a connection with the Supreme. The theta state is when you are connected with God and are beginning to receive his light and might. The delta state comes about when the mind is completely quiet and you are deep in the experience of God's light and God's love. You don't need to have a conscious thought or to label or describe the experience. You are simply in a state of beingness. This is the state that has been described as the state of connectedness with the whole world – when we have this empathy with the whole world we create a state in which healing takes place.

All this research is amazing! But how do you get there? How do you make it happen? How do you take charge and say, 'This is where I want to go and this is how I am going to do it?'

This book shows you how – and it is a very simple process. The first step is to be soul-conscious. This is the state in which we start creating thoughts that are positive and related to truth and reality.

Then, when we begin to meditate we create the thought that 'I am a soul; I am a child of God.'

When we think about the external world, the mind moves very fast. When we think about our own inner world then the speed of our thoughts automatically slows down. The very technique of meditation contained in this book teaches us to think in the right way. And we don't just learn to think in the right way while meditating for ten minutes a day. This technique teaches us to think in the right way ALL the time.

Introduction

We think of ourselves as human beings, but have you ever thought about the dual aspects of this phrase? On one side we have the human element, and on the other side the being. The 'human' side of us is made up by the body – and we know a huge amount about the body since volumes of books, thousands of medical schools and millions of internet pages are dedicated to its study. It's easy to find the answer to any question you might have about the body. But how much do we really know about the other side of what we are: the 'being'?

Thinking about being

At its most elemental, we can say that the body is limited by space and time, and that its form will lose its shape when we die. We can also draw a recognisable image of a body on a piece of paper. It is much more difficult to describe what the being is at its most elemental, or to draw a picture of it.

We can't draw the being as an image because it is abstract, or subtle. In Raja Yoga we describe the being as a point of light – like a star radiating light. That is what the 'being' part of us is. Light is energy, and the energy of the being drives the body. We might think of the brain in the body like the engine of a car – it has immense potential power – and we might think of food as the fuel that powers that engine. But can a car function without a driver? No. In the same way, the body cannot function without a being to drive it. I am the being in my body, and I am the being that makes this body function.

Why do we say this?

We could talk for hours about the many different aspects of the body – we could investigate the brain and circulatory system, for example, the cells and nerves – but none of this will give us any indication as to who we really are. I find it useful to think of myself like a sea creature in a shell; the shell is simply a place in which the creature lives. The creature is inside, and the shell is on the outside. Similarly, the body is only the outer cover of the place where I, the being, live. The being is inside, it is everything I am, but is never visible.

How can we begin to see this inner being?

Though this inner being is invisible, we can tune into it. A good place to start is by looking at our thoughts. Think about how thoughts come and go. I can scarcely catch all my thoughts as there are so many. Think, too, about where they go – it is impossible to know how many places our thoughts whizz to. Have you ever sat with a pen and paper writing something? Suddenly your hand stops writing. You are gone for some moments, and only minutes later does your consciousness return to awareness of the present moment and the task in hand. So where did you go? Maybe as you were writing, you were suddenly reminded of a childhood experience, or maybe your thoughts became tied up in all the things you have to do tomorrow. Maybe you travelled around the world or even went back in time! Your mind is capable of travelling everywhere in a moment; to the mind there are no barriers of past or future, would have been or yet might be. The mind is able to transcend both time and space.

Distance provides no barrier to our thoughts either. I can think about the fire station just next door to my house, about a bus stop down the road or about New York and instantly be there. It takes me exactly the same amount of time to think about next door, down the road or New York. So distance as well as time is no barrier to our thoughts. This just proves how powerful the mind is – and how boundless this invisible inner being is.

Beyond time and space

Sometimes thoughts come to us from the world outside ourselves – you might say something, for example, and I will respond to it. Sometimes I am sitting here and my mind disappears somewhere – as it did when I stopped writing a moment ago to follow my thoughts. When this happens, you might look at me and say, 'Hey are you still with me?' That outside stimulus then triggers the thoughts in my brain to turn back to my present surroundings.

The brain is just hardware. It has a location in time and space; it is physical. Of course, the brain is immensely valuable and incredibly powerful, but it is still situated within the physical domain. Because the brain is made of matter, it is part of the body. A medic or scientist can dissect and examine the brain and draw conclusions from its physicality. The more intricate the surgeon's instrument, the more deeply he is able to explore its physicality and functions, but nevertheless, he can only look into its physical structure.

So the brain is physical, but things that are physical are not able to create things that lie beyond the physical. If my thoughts are beyond time and space, then my brain cannot be creating those thoughts. There is a contradiction in this thought: the brain exists in the here and now, but my thoughts are not constrained by time and distance. I can quite easily imagine a situation that has never happened and possibly never will. Writers of science fiction, philosophers and quantum physicists do it all the time.

Beyond weight and width

Feelings are an essential part of what defines us as human beings. And feelings, too, exist in a realm beyond time and space or distance. If I think back to a particular event in my childhood, then all the feelings that I experienced at that time start to well up in me in the present, whether they are pleasant or not so pleasant. If I imagine my life in ten years' time and think about where I might live or what my role might be at that moment, different emotions emerge – feelings of fear and anxiety, perhaps, intermingled with anticipation and hope start to overtake me. This experience demonstrates how far our feelings lie beyond time and space. So too does our ability to visualise and choose, to have an attitude and ideals, faith and awareness, intentions and memories, and our ability to hope and to discern truth.

Meditation is the tool that makes us aware of these more subtle aspects of the inner self. When we meditate we become aware of all these qualities – and many more – and eventually recognise that they emanate from inside us. Even though these spiritual and metaphysical aspects are invisible, they make me who I am. All of them are contained within the 'being' part of me, which is non-physical and imperishable, unlike the physical body. And these subtle aspects of my being are what make me absolutely unique.

How am I unique?

Let's think more about why each of us is completely unique. We are not just defined by the particular eye or hair colour we have and whichever other physical characteristics we inherited from our parents. Our physical being is completely different from every other human being. But so is the invisible part of us that makes up our 'being'. Let's take our intellect and memory as an example. The intellect of one person is quite different from the intellect of anyone else. My intellect includes my values, which have been created in turn by the influences of my culture, my education, my parents and my friends – all those influences are unique to me. Our memories are also quite different from one another – obviously, given that we have all travelled different paths. In addition, there are also differences in how we remember a shared situation, or an event that many people have been involved in. This is not just because we have differences in perspective, it is also because each one of us has a unique capacity to recall or remember that event. And as such, we will remember things quite differently from one another. For example, the lesson that each of us carries away, holds in our thoughts and remembers from reading this book will be very, very different from every other reader – it will be unique.

All of this uniqueness is contained within my – and your – being, the point of radiant luminous light that we are. A point is without length, width, breadth or height – it exists, but it exists outside of any of these measurements. In the same way I, like you, am just a point, and within this point there is no weight or any other physical element, only living energy. This point of living energy is located just in front of the brain and it works through the brain. By using the brain, this point of energy executes everything that needs to happen in order to send out and receive information. I am this unique being – the soul that has within it all these amazing things – all the time. But only by turning inwards during meditation do I learn to see and appreciate the amazing inner being that I truly am.

Lesson 1

PREPARING FOR MEDITATION

Before we begin to meditate – and to appreciate the point of light that each of us is – we need to learn to relax. In this relaxation exercise, we will teach the brain what it means to relax, and help the physical body to let go of unhelpful tension.

Relaxation means asking the body to do nothing, and both the body and brain find that rather puzzling at first! It's like saying 'Everybody, now picture *not* pink.' So what do you picture? *Pink!* In Raja Yoga we often use such 'negations'; we use words such as 'incorporeal', which means 'not physical'. This way of speaking and thinking keeps the intellect active. In the example above, for instance, first your brain says 'OK, I know pink' but then it is forced to adjust to contemplate the more abstract idea 'not pink'. Similarly, when asked to 'do nothing', the brain and body have to fight the urge to do something before beginning to relax into the more abstract 'nothing'. Spirituality is that abstract, too; it needs to be *experienced* and that takes time.

When we start meditating, the first problem we encounter is our natural intelligence. We are so clever that we think we understand. This hinders our spiritual growth. It is better to come to meditation with a less knowing attitude, thinking, 'I don't understand everything, but this is exciting and I am going to find out'. Then your journey into meditation will be both enjoyable and help you to progress in your life.

Sitting comfortably

Let us begin our first journey towards meditation with some silence. Sit comfortably in a chair with your feet flat on the floor. Take everything off your lap, uncross your legs and just relax your hands on your lap. Try to keep your eyes open; rest your eyes on something still and blink naturally, but consciously just be here.

Now I want you to clench your right fist as tightly as you can and really focus on relaxing your left hand. Clench your right hand and really relax your left hand. Don't move your left hand – that is the opposite of relaxation and introduces tension; just relax your hand.

Do you feel an unusual lightness in your left hand? That is your brain working out what relaxation means. It is a nervous response. We are reprogramming the nervous system, which right now only knows what 'action' means; it doesn't know what 'to relax' means.

Now completely relax your right hand and really tighten your left hand. Swap it over, really relaxing your left hand again and clenching your right hand. Your brain is starting to learn what relaxation feels like. Swap over your hands again. Really relax that right hand. Now let go of your left hand as well. Let all the tension go and record the feeling and sensation of what it is like to let everything go. Just notice it – see how deliberate it is? Meditation is a deliberate process, too.

Relaxing the feet and legs

Now we have instructed the brain using the hands, let us do the same by letting go of tension in the feet. In the same way that you let go of tension in your hands, let go of your feet. Don't move them – this just creates tension and a sense-memory of tension. Just let your feet go – abandon them. Sense that same lightness of being in your feet. Do you feel it? It is a funny feeling of nervousness. You will know when you have fully let your feet go because you will feel no difference between the floor and your feet. In other words, the interface between the floor and your feet will disappear. It will feel as if your ankles are the end of your body.

Don't worry if you experience other sensations or thoughts. All kinds of things will crop up during these relaxation exercises; some emotions may come out, some pains may make themselves known – but this is normal and nothing to worry about. So completely let go of your feet. Keep your eyes open though.

Let go of your legs now. Try not to move them – just let go of all the tension. Keep your focus entirely on yourself and your body. Now let go of your pelvis, your buttocks and all the muscles around your lower back as well. Let go of those muscles and the tension associated with them. You are the one who holds the tension and you can let it go, too. You proved this with your hands – you clenched your fists and you let the tension go. So now let go of the muscles in your lower back. You are a spirit and you are completely free. Let it go.

Letting go of the upper body

Let go of all the tension in your upper back now, then focus on your stomach and let all the tension there go too. Breathe in through your nose and out through your mouth. Breathe in again, and as you exhale through your mouth, breathe out *all* your tension.

Releasing the chest

Let go of your chest now by breathing into the whole region. Breathe in through your nose and out through your mouth. Breathe in through your nose right into your chest and let the tension out through your mouth.

Here – now – is the only moment that exists. Be just you, free in the now, letting go of tension in your chest and you breathe into your chest through your nose and out through your mouth.

Abandon your arms

Let go of your hands now. Don't move them; just abandon them – let them go. Let go of your arms. Let go of your shoulders, allowing them to drop downwards. Breathe into your shoulders through your nose and let out the tension in your arms and shoulders as you exhale through your mouth…

Release and relax

Let go of your neck now. It helps to release your jaw and your tongue again. If you find your mouth naturally falls open, let it. Let it all go.

Let go of tension in your scalp now as you exhale, and imagine the 150 muscles in your face softening and relaxing. Try to keep your eyes open as you relax your face, which helps you to stay really alert and present while you become totally detached and relaxed.

You are not your body

Now let go of all your facial muscles. Smooth out any frown lines on your forehead and imagine your temples softening. Let go of the muscles behind your eyes. Leave your eyes open but let them relax absolutely. Let go of your cheekbones, and all the muscles behind your cheeks, along your jaw and around your mouth.

Silently ask yourself, 'Who let go of this body?' The answer is 'I did'. So who are you? Answering 'I did' means you are not your body. You are the one who let go of your body. So who are you? You are the intelligence reading and following the instructions – you have let go of your whole body. You are the loving beautiful energy made of light – you are light energy, you are consciousness.

Now I want you to think of yourself as a concentrated light energy. Anything concentrated is powerful, like the sun. The sun is concentrated energy; a star in the night sky is concentrated energy, too. Now visualise yourself as a star, like those you see in the night sky. You are just a tiny spark – visualise that – like a spark of sunlight on the water; like a sparkling diamond.

A point of light

By focusing and visualising, bring your mental energy to a tiny point. Notice how you begin to experience a well of peace – feel the breeze of peace sweeping through you.

Feel silence, peace and relaxation. Say to yourself silently, 'I am a tiny pinpoint or spark of light. I am not this body, but I am the one who moves this body. I am the one who lives in this body. I am the awareness; I am a soul, the life energy and the life force in this body. I am peaceful'.

Come back into an awareness of the room around you. You will feel slightly detached but filled with love. The power of silence builds up in you in this way every time you meditate, creating a reservoir of energy and the ability to feel quite detached from a situation, but full of love.

Use your body again by moving in your chair. See how relaxed you are. Do you feel light? Try to retain awareness of this lightness and complete relaxation as you go about your day.

Meditation

Sitting comfortably in silence, I let my body become calm and quiet and I journey inward.

I have come here to see the self, to experience the self and to experience attainment. So I look inside. In order to get to know myself very, very well, I must ask myself the question, 'Who am I?' many, many times today. Every time I ask myself 'Who am I?' I will experience positive change.

Let me be able to know myself. Let my thoughts become very, very pure – this is the way to find the treasures within me that I have forgotten about. There I will also find the desire to share my treasures – of love, compassion, faith and honesty – with others.

I enter into the silence. If we develop a habit, we automatically remember how to do it, so I will develop the habit of going inside myself today.

At first, it seems a little difficult to look at myself. But once I develop the practice, I will find that turning inward makes all external problems seem easy. There is then no tension and no pressure. I feel liberated from old habits and free from the influence of others. I understand what to do and how to do it.

I turn inward and see how everything becomes easy.

Point summary

- Before we begin to meditate, we need to bring the body to the state of relaxation.
- Spirituality is very subtle and needs to be experienced instead of just being talked about.
- Preparing yourself for meditation involves letting go of the tension of the body as well as our "knowing" attitude and personal views.
- Understand that you are not your body nor your thoughts and feelings. You are the consciousness, the light energy who lives in this body, the one who moves this body.

Self-reflective question:

What are the benefits of meditation on physical, mental and spiritual levels?

Self-experimentation

At least four times a day, spend a few minutes to consciously practise using the mind to relax the body. Once the body is relaxed, bring your mental attention to the light energy in the centre of your forehead, and experience the state of inner peace. Speak to your mind, "I am the awareness, the soul, the life force in this body. I am peaceful".

Lesson 2
ALL ABOUT THE SOUL

The soul contains within it three faculties – the mind, the intellect and our personality traits. Meditation introduces us to these three aspects of ourselves and shows us how to explore them further. Let's now look at each one in turn.

The mind

The mind has two different functions. First, it has the ability to create thoughts. In fact the mind is constantly creating a never-ending stream of thoughts. It is like a machine with amazing energy, churning out thoughts non-stop. According to an interview with Dr. Dennis Gersten, who is certified by the American Board of Psychiatry and Neurology, the average person has around 15,000 thoughts per day, and at least half of them are negative. Other research has suggested that we have even more thoughts if we are worried about something that has happened or are anticipating or fearful of something that might happen in the distant future or is about to happen later in the day.

The second function of the mind is to create feelings. When we talk about our feelings, we often sense them around our physical heart – this is why we often put our hands on our chests as we talk about how good or bad we are feeling. When we talk about our feelings we talk about the heart – so where is the heart, and how is it connected with the mind and the soul?

Of course, the machine that pumps blood around our veins is located in the body. Surgeons can do amazing things with this muscular pump, the heart. They can pull it out and repair it, or put in a machine that replaces part of its function; they can even take out someone else's heart and connect it into a different body. So the feelings we associate with the heart cannot reside in this physical heart, which circulates blood around the body. Our feelings instead reside within the soul, the living part of our being. Feelings are a quality of life; part of our living being. We experience thoughts and emotions within the soul; the body is simply the means by which we experience them.

So how do our feelings connect with our thoughts? Firstly the mind creates thoughts and then those thoughts become our feelings. So our thoughts and feelings are connected. If I have thoughts connected to complaining then I will feel frustrated and irritated; on the other hand, if I have peaceful thoughts I will feel calm and uplifted. My thoughts go through a pattern of changes and turn into feelings. Thoughts can change quickly, but feelings tend to be slower to respond. For example, I can recall the feelings I had in a certain situation in the past long after the actual thoughts that generated those feelings have been forgotten.

Some people say that feelings just come to us. For example we might say, 'You made me so unhappy because you said this and this', or we might say, 'You made me so happy today'. We associate our feelings with what is coming to us from 'out there'. But this is not correct. The truth is that I can choose how I wish to respond to what you say to me – and I make that choice from within me, using my intellect. The intellect is truly the lord and master of the mind. But if we stop using the intellect then the mind will become habitually reactive and it will seem as if I am allowing the self to be manipulated by people and situations outside myself.

Meditation

I sit comfortably in silence and relax my body.

In order to experience peace, I have to be totally free from the demands of ego. I chose to release myself from my daily activities and commitments, to let go worry about how much there is to do. I leave behind the feeling of having to do this and that. I liberate myself from the influence of sorrow, pain and fear. Becoming wise means freeing myself from these three things.

Sometimes there seems no place to escape from what is going on in the world. But there is a place: the space of my innermost self. I can do my inner work wherever I am. Wherever I go I carry my own baggage around with me, the burdens and memories of the past. And if I don't do my inner work, I will still be carrying that baggage when it is time to leave this life. Great souls like Mahatma Gandhi and Mother Theresa did their 'work' while alive, and now have left their bodies. But the legacy of their elevated actions remains as a memorial to them.

Let me not just look at the goodness of others, but also be inspired by them, let me personally make effort to do something for the world. Let me serve the world and give happiness to everyone. If I clean my heart then compassion, honesty and love are able to emerge and do their work. The mind is then liberated from mischief; it becomes released from the burden of desires and therefore strong and free.

All I need is to discipline my mind to create fewer thoughts – elevated thoughts - and then there can be peace inside.

When my mind is peaceful, I feel love. I become the embodiment of love. The love of a peaceful mind is able to reach others. It touches the hearts of others. Then the soul feels happy all the time, and nothing can reduce that happiness within. The soul becomes independent – free. If I need to look for happiness outside myself, I am not free, but dependent. Let me become free... internally. Let me experience freedom inside. Let me have such a connection with the Divine that I am able to take unlimited happiness and share it with everyone.

By understanding myself and making my mind peaceful, I am able to feel love; when I experience happiness my power begins to increase. All this begins with the process of looking inside and cleansing the self. Then Peace follows, and I experience happiness and peace.

The intellect

This is the second part of the soul. In Hindi it is referred to as *buddhi*. The process of meditation helps us to strengthen the intellect. A strong intellect equips us to choose which thoughts we want to have – and by changing our thoughts we are able to change our feelings. Then we can respond to people and situations instead of merely reacting out of habit to them. The intellect has two very specific abilities.

Firstly, it has the capacity for understanding. It's useful to imagine the intellect as being like a receptacle: a container that holds information. We are surrounded and bombarded by so much information today. There is no way we can hold all of it in our minds, and so we select and retain only what is useful – though maybe a few useless things stay with us, too! Our intellect extracts from that information the knowledge that is useful for us as individuals to use in our unique lives, and then stores it, like a container. If my intellect retains spiritual knowledge, for example, that becomes useful for me in my life and, as I use that knowledge, this way of thinking becomes my experience. Then that knowledge becomes wisdom. As I begin to follow the path of wisdom, I begin to move in the direction of truth. So, my intellect has the capacity to lead me towards truth. The mind may go here and there and everywhere, but my intellect remains my compass.

The second capacity of the intellect, after understanding, is the ability to sense right and wrong – my intellect is not only my moral compass, it is my conscience, too. If the knowledge that I hold in my intellect and work with is knowledge I understand and believe in, it will determine the way in which my conscience works. That will impact on all the decisions I make in my life. So my intellect contains my capacity to discriminate, understand and decide upon action.

Up until this moment – for most of us anyway – our understanding of ourselves has been along the following lines: I am this body, I am male, I am female, I am Indian, I am British, I am from the Caribbean. Or it has focused on our professions – I am a doctor, manager, teacher – or on our relationships – I am a mother, father, sister and so on. Because this is the understanding I have held in my intellect, this is the understanding that has formed my belief system. Those beliefs have then impacted on all the decisions I have made because my understanding and my beliefs determine my decisions. Logic, reasoning, understanding and analysis are all part of the intellect. However, that part of the intellect that reflects my values, attitudes and motives is my conscience and my conscience has an impact on all of these. My mind flits around here and there and so is not part of my reasoning. Reasoning, evaluating and decision-making is the job of the intellect.

Meditation

I sit comfortably in silence and relax my body.

I imagine a transparent sphere. It represents my consciousness. The inner surface of the sphere represents my mind – a screen that extends all around me, the 'self-aware self'. Inside, at the centre of the sphere, is a ball of light. This represents my spiritual heart, the core of my being.

To connect my heart centre to my thinking faculties, I use my intellect, the power centre of decision-making and judgement. In this silent space of the inner self I am able to make use of the full range of my higher thinking. I can discern when to use my mind in a rational process of 'thinking things through' so that I achieve clarity – a clear vision displayed on the screen of my mind.

And I can discern when the 'self-aware self' may turn toward the heart of my being, that central core of wisdom where I make use of my intuition, my intuitive feelings and deep knowing.

I 'the self-aware self', can move easily between these two modes during the day, using my intellect in either way. I can choose to use the 'rational mode', which tends to require a great deal of thought generation (possibility thinking) or I can use the 'intuitive mode' which tends to require a quiet mind so that I have a clearer awareness of what I perceive or feel at a deeper or more subtle level. I will practise this today.

Personality traits

Our personality traits make up the third and final aspect of the soul. In Hindi we call these our *sanskaras*. Let me define this term very simply: *sanskaras* are all the experiences I have been through in life. They have accumulated within me and have shaped my personality. For example, I was born in India, so the experience of the Indian way of life, language and culture has shaped me since birth. I was educated in London so, similarly, that experience shaped me later in my youth. Wherever I have travelled and wherever I have worked I have gathered experiences, which accumulated within the self and have created what my personality is today.

If any sections of those life experiences were missing from my past, then my personality today would be different. If I had been born in a different country, spoken a different language, grown up in a different city, worked in different situations – all of those different experiences would have shaped me and would have made me quite different from what I am today. If you look at my face you will see wrinkles on my forehead and grey hair, but it is impossible for you physically to see the experiences I have been through. However, all of them are recorded within me – within this tiny point of light that forms the soul – and how those experiences have influenced me impacts on everything I do.

How is my attitude shaped?

All the experiences recorded within the self have not just shaped who I am today but have forged my perceptions, beliefs and attitudes. I create beliefs based on the influences of my life, and from these beliefs my opinions emerge. These will, in turn, determine my attitudes. For instance, if I were bitten by a dog when I was a toddler, then my attitude towards dogs may be one of fear. But if in my childhood I grew up with a lovely puppy that adored me and followed me wherever I went, that experience would be recorded in me, too. So even if that creature died many years ago, my beloved pet shaped my world-view of dogs, and today whenever I see a dog my attitude towards it will be one of friendliness, without fear. All our attitudes to everything will have been shaped by the experiences that have been recorded within us. And these things are, incredibly, all held within this point of light, the soul.

If I have to perform a routine task every day and my past experience is one of dislike for that task, I will allow myself to develop an attitude of dislike and I will probably put off doing the task for as long as possible. But if I can develop a different attitude – of patience, perhaps, or determination – towards that task, it will lose its power to generate dislike in me. The awareness that I can change a situation by changing my attitude comes from knowing myself through meditation.

The reason why we need to understand all this is because we work with these different aspects of the self in meditation. In Raja Yoga we are not concerned with whether you can sit crossed-legged or not, and we are not going to teach you how to sit cross-legged. Neither are we going to teach you breathing exercises, which are of course beneficial, but are not what Raja Yoga meditation is about. Instead, we are showing you how to get to know the only aspect that really matters – the divine soul. When your mind is focused, your breathing will quite naturally become calm, and you will be able to feel a difference in your body. When you are excited and nervous what is your breathing like? When you are soul-conscious and centred there is an automatic impact on your breathing, then the body comes into a state of total relaxation in which all the tension and the pressures that have accumulated within you are released. You do not have to force the body and train your mind. You start with attention on your mind and then naturally you find that you are able to establish the comfort and harmony that your body requires to find inner peace.

Meditation

I sit comfortably in silence and look inside myself.

I begin by imagining my thinking, my whole thought process, as a tree.

I can view my perception and my established belief patterns as the roots of a tree, deep below the surface of my conscious thoughts. Rising from them, like the trunk of this tree, are my thinking habits and recurrent feelings. From these grow my actions, the branches of the tree. And sprouting out from those actions are all the little variations, twigs of habit that develop as time goes on.

The tree of my personality grows as time passes; my thoughts and feelings and actions gradually become farther and farther away from that seed that was my original self. As I sit in silent reflection, in meditation, I go deeper into my awareness, into my understanding, deep into this root-level of the subconscious. This is where change can take place, where old long-held beliefs can be altered or eradicated.

From this quiet place of understanding, I can take the opportunity to examine my behaviour, my old habits one by one. And focussing on each one in turn, looking back into memory and beyond, I can try to identify what belief lies beneath each and its root.

Gently and gradually, through silence and reflection I can begin to visualise how I would like the tree of my personality to develop and grow.

Point summary

- The soul contains within it three faculties – the mind, the intellect and our personality traits.

  - The functions of the mind are to create thoughts and feelings. As is our thought, so is our feeling.
  - The intellect (the Buddhi) has the capacity for understanding, reasoning, evaluating and making decisions.
  - Our personality traits (Sanskaras) carry all the experiences the soul has been through whereby personal tendencies and personality traits are impressed on the soul.

- Feelings are a quality of life. We experience thoughts and emotions within the soul; the body is the means by which we experience them.

- The process of meditation is to strengthen the intellect and to understand the relationship between your mind, your intellect and your personality traits.

Self-reflective question:

What is attitude and how does it impact on the decisions I make in my life?

Self-experimentation

In meditation and even whilst you carry out actions, bring the self to the point of self-awareness, and experiment with the three faculties: create a thought in the mind, focus on that one thought, and use the intellect to discriminate if it is a beneficial thought. If you decide there is no benefit, let go of the thought and create a good thought. Be aware if the thought draws out any other thoughts and feelings from your memories. If so, stay detached and let them go.

Lesson 3
KNOWING MYSELF

The first steps in meditation are all about getting to know ourselves. So far we have explored only the very basics – knowing what is going on in the soul, this point of light. Now, the aim of our meditation is to go deeper and deeper and deeper within ourselves. Superficial thoughts tend to occupy the mind – thoughts about the material world of here and now and of everything going on around us in the mundane world. In this chapter we will start bypassing those mundane thoughts and delving a bit deeper so that you begin to see what your true beliefs are. We will start our investigation by asking a fundamental question about our beliefs. Ask yourself this: 'Do I believe I am a body?'

When I believe I am a body then the way I think, see and act is very materialistic. The body is made of matter and so if I believe that I am a body then it puts me into a materialistic compartment, in which all my aims, my goals and my values are connected with the material world, and this world alone. If I am a materialist then I am not able to remain happy all the time because I will suffer a great deal of fear about the possibility of losing anything I own. The fear is generated by all the things that are external to the self because I cannot control circumstances or other people. For example, think about buying a fantastic new car. Obviously, having a new car would bring about a great deal of happiness, but we cannot prevent someone from vandalising the car and spoiling that happiness. So once we have that car, we will be consciously or unconsciously living with a certain level of fear.

If I am aware that I am a spiritual being, then my intellect has the understanding and the belief that I am a soul. The big paradigm shift happens when instead of thinking I am this body, I come to the awareness that I am a point of light – I am a soul. When I truly believe that I am a soul things change on all levels: the way I look at things, what I say, the way I act, the way I interact, the way I perceive and the way my attitude is. There is a total shift. All of this is within the soul already, and so as I go deeper within myself during meditation I first see my thoughts, then I see my beliefs and, as I go deeper still, I see my personality traits. I see what lies below the surface – what I really am.

This can be a very depressing exercise! It can put many of us off meditation at first because for most of us, the experiences we have been through in the recent past may not have been very uplifting. Maybe there have been a few positive moments here and there, but generally speaking the memories most of us carry – and the imprints most of us carry – come from experiencing sorrow, anger, guilt or fear.

Discovering peace

The reality is that the original personality trait of the soul is of peace. Peace is who I am. When I begin to come to that awareness of peace through meditation – understanding that peace is my true nature – my heart starts to feel comfortable and it begins to open up so that the next experience I encounter is one of love. In peace I can come back to the loving self that I truly am.

When I am peaceless, that love disappears! But when I return to a peaceful state I come back to an experience of love. Love is part of the soul. This spiritual love is not conditional upon anything external to the self. It is nurturing and supportive and can uplift others because of its purity of motive. Spiritual love is not dependent on the love of another because it is a natural way of being.

Understanding truth

When we look deep inside through meditation, we come to another experience, too – one of truth. They say that all answers are there within us. It is true! Let yourself become very quiet and peaceful as you sit to meditate, then let your heart be very open and loving and you will begin to gain a glimpse of truth. Whatever falsehoods and illusions you have acquired and have been hanging on to begin to dissolve as you come to an awareness of truth. Truth is reality. Truth is eternal, unchanging, constant, immutable and universal, and we start to recognise the truth about the self once we become aware of our own original state of being, which is purity.

Purity has become influenced by everything that has been going on outside us, but the original state of every soul is one of purity. Purity is freedom from all negativity. The original and natural state of the soul is not one of sorrow, anger, guilt or fear, it is one of happiness, and happiness emerges naturally when we are free from all that negativity. True happiness is not the happiness of a pleasurable turn of events, but is a constant companion independent of what is going on in the world around us.

As we move onto the path of spirituality and discover our original *sanskaras*, or personality traits, and realise those experiences, we come to another very beautiful experience – we experience our own inner power.

Inner power

When we are unhappy, we feel hopeless in that moment, and lose all sense of being powerful. When we are under the influence of all sorts of illusions that come from outside the self we also lose our power and begin to feel like a victim. We have the sense that everything is pushing us down. Let's look at these illusions a little further. We have created expectations based on the illusions that come from the external influences in our lives and how we perceive them – from parents and peers and from the influence of our gender, appearance, education, culture and the media, to name but a few. All these influences have created within us the illusion that we are this body and because they come from outside the self, we look outside ourselves for approval. We become dependent on respect from the outside and from others in order to feel worthy, rather than understanding that self-respect is self-generated. Our self-esteem is dependent when it is based on how others see us. Because of this external focus, our own internal well-being remains in a constant state of flux. One moment we blossom, but the next we wilt, and when we wilt we can feel hopeless and not very powerful at all. But when we come back to the experience of our original state of being, we experience tremendous inner power. Meditation allows us to spend time in our original state, which restores our inner power. Let us experiment with this by spending a few minutes in silence following this guided meditation. When we sit in silence we can come back to the core of the being that we are and connect with all the treasures within us. In the following practical exercise you use the mind in a very positive and active way to connect with your own inner being. This is meditation.

Meditation

Sitting comfortably in silence, I let my body become calm and quiet and I journey inward. I become aware of the being that I am – the soul. I am the shining star in the centre of my forehead... this is who I am... this body is the vehicle that I have taken to experience life, but now I go on the journey within. I see my thoughts, but I want to go deeper... I go deeper within... and I see the beliefs that I hold and the faith that I have. I now believe... I have the faith that I am a soul, an eternal and immortal being.

I go even deeper within the self... and I discover the stillness at the core of my being. Within myself there is peace. I am a being of peace... and in this awareness my heart opens up and I realise that what I am most comfortable with is the state of love. When other things intrude, I do not feel comfortable... I want to clean out all other feelings so that I can return within – to the warmth, the security and the reality of my natural state of love. Peace and love begin to give me a glimpse of truth... I begin to see what is real and what is true – that which is forever.

As I shed the illusions and falsehood, I feel clean... the dust is being washed away. The power of love has cleansed me... and so my natural state begins to sparkle... my natural state is one of purity, peace, love and truth. I feel so content that my contentment brings me great joy. This is who I am... my natural state is one of happiness. All these treasures are there within me and now that I remember who I am, I am filled with joy.

Not only is this my experience, but this experience spills over and impacts on everyone around me... I become an instrument for sharing peace, love, happiness, truth and purity in all directions.

Holding this awareness and experience, I come back to the moment here in this room, aware of the things in the physical dimension but now the light is shining bright in the centre of my forehead.

Point summary

- Within the soul are five original qualities– peace, purity, truth, love, and bliss all belong to us. When we realise ourselves as souls, we can experience these inner qualities.

- Our fear is generated by trying to control external circumstances.

- During meditation, as we go deep we see our thoughts, beliefs, our personality traits; and what lies below the surface –the pure being that I really am.

- Meditation allows us to spend time in the awareness of our original state, shedding all falsehood and illusions, restoring our inner power.

Difference between true and false self:

I am a soul Soul Consciousness	I am this body Body Consciousness
Understanding of self as a spiritual being	Understanding of self as a physical being
I, the soul, am playing many different roles	I am what I play in my roles.
Values connected to self-respect	Values connected to the material world
Ability to detach from roles, separating thought from emotion	Fear of not being able to control external circumstances or other people
Experience of freedom and lightness	Experience of dependency and heaviness

Self-reflective question:

What is the truth about the self? What are the difficulties in realising the self as an eternal being?

Self-experimentation

Set aside a place and a time to meditate. Early morning before the start of the day is preferable. During meditation, create a quiet space in your mind beyond all thoughts, feelings and emotions. In this space you can build up a stock of silence which you can tap into during the day. It is an inner sanctuary, a meditation room in your mind. During the day, practise speaking less often, and speaking more softly.

Lesson 4

THE IMPACT OF OUR THOUGHTS AND ACTIONS

There is another aspect of the human and the being that we need to investigate – the relationship between the soul and the body. On the path of spirituality the relationship between soul and body is very important, so we need to understand how it works. We can use meditation to find out about the aspect of the self that acts in the world – this helps us to understand how the energy of the soul is used in different ways. This is a valuable lesson to learn, especially in relation to the way we act in the world and the quality of our actions. We will begin by thinking about the word *karma*.

The Hindi word *karma* simply means 'action'. Our thoughts lead us into action. And our actions impact in two ways. Firstly there is the impact our actions have on the outside world. When I do something, it has an impact on you. If I give you flowers, my action has an impact. If I give you a cup of tea, there is an impact. If I throw a stone at you, there is an impact.

If I speak words that are not inspiring and encouraging but instead are hurtful and harmful, there is an impact.

Secondly, the impact of our action leaves an imprint on the self. Our actions have an impact not only out there but also on the self. Whatever I choose to do has an impact on me also.

Earlier we looked at how our *sanskaras*, or personality traits, are composed of the sum total of our experiences, but these experiences are a result of our actions. Every time I perform an action, the *sanskara* becomes firmer. I give you a flower as an expression of kindness, love or compassion, and so the *sanskaras* underlined within myself are of the same nature: of love, kindness and compassion. So the next time I see you, the same thoughts come to mind and I want to express that love. But if instead I speak roughly to you, my *sanskara* becomes firm in that way and so next time I see you, I don't even think twice, I just automatically speak to you in the same dismissive way. In this way, stone-throwing and harmful words become a way of life.

Cyclical behaviour

When our cycle of thoughts, actions and *sanskaras* is on a positive track – one of goodness, kindness and compassion – life is good for all of us. But often today, the world impacts on us in a very negative way. This is because although we have deep within us our original *sanskaras* – of peace, truth and purity – we also have the acquired *sanskaras* of a little greed, ego, anger and attachment. We are thoroughly mixed up. Generally speaking, today the world does not impact on us in a compassionate way. Compassion isn't rewarded – force and anger are rewarded, and so they grow within us.

Because the *sanskaras* that we carry are a bit mixed up – combining anger and ego for example with our original truth and purity – our thoughts follow the same pattern and our actions reflect our thoughts. So every time we perform an action, our *sanskaras* are underlined again and again and the habit becomes entrenched. When challenged about our negativity or difficult behaviour we respond,' What can I do? This is my nature. This is just how I am.' That is not how we were originally; it is how we have developed by habitually repeating actions in the same old way.

How to change this pattern

The cycle of thoughts, actions and *sanskaras* becomes a vicious trap. Thoughts turn into action, and every time we perform that action, the *sanskaras* become more firmly set. In a similar way our *sanskaras* emerge as a thought, which leads to an action, and that action reinforces the *sanskaras* still further.

To change this pattern of *sanskaras* I have to remember a significant aspect of human nature: before thoughts can become actions we have to let the intellect in on the act, by using our inbuilt understanding and our natural sense of right and wrong. This will tell us whether we should or should not carry out that action. How will we know whether the action is right or wrong? When, during meditation, I am in the awareness that I am a soul, I can always discern right from wrong because the qualities of the soul are those of peace, love and wisdom. If I remain in that awareness, I will know which action is right.

So, if we decide that an action is wrong and don't carry it through, then that's it; problem solved! Unfortunately, it doesn't quite work that easily. Sometimes we bypass the intellect completely. We don't take a moment to pause and ask, 'Should I or should I not perform that action?' We instantly engage in action and only afterward have to deal with realisation, regret and repentance.

We tend to ignore the intellect and go ahead and put a thought into action even when the intellect shouts, 'Don't do it!' I may decide, for example, to give up smoking, but when I wake in the morning I automatically reach for my first cigarette. Only after smoking most of it do I realise what I have done. The bad habit is so ingrained that the intellect was bypassed completely.

Meditation: the key to success

It is because the intellect has become this dysfunctional that we need to meditate. The intellect has become weak from lack of use in the same way that muscles become weak when we neglect to take regular exercise. The first step in flexing the intellect's muscles is to keep coming back to an awareness of the soul. In the awareness of the soul, I connect with my own inner peace and then the world out there can't ruffle me.

The second key is to understand this circle of thoughts, intellect, actions and *sanskaras*. It is important not to allow thoughts to emerge straight into action, but instead, to switch on the filter of my intellect so that only that which is true and right emerges into action.

If we allow our thoughts to emerge directly as action we will never gain control over them because thoughts can be wild! We all know how the mind works; all sorts of thoughts come to it: negative thoughts, wasteful thoughts, weak thoughts and even awful thoughts. When we start working with spiritual understanding – being aware of being a soul – we experience pure thoughts, noble thoughts and elevated thoughts because we are connected with our original *sanskaras* of peace, love, purity and happiness. When we forget to switch on the intellect, all sorts of negative thoughts come in to interrupt our natural state of awareness.

If my intellect has spoken to me a few times and I have ignored it a few times, it will stop speaking to me. I will no longer realise whether I am doing something right or wrong. Then the actions I perform lack that filter of conscience and negative *sanskaras* easily take over and become reinforced.

Morality and meditation

There are three states of being in the world. In the first we inhabit a state in which morality, values and the highest *sanskaras* are enacted and we use them to direct our actions. We call this way of life moral. Then there is a second state in which we know what is right and what is wrong but don't have the power to follow the correct course of action. Although the morals, ethics and values are within us, we have moved away from them. We describe that world as being immoral.

But there is a third state in which the conscience has totally gone to sleep and is no longer making itself heard. When this happens we are not even aware that one choice is right and the other is wrong – there is denial instead. When we live in a state of denial we say, 'Anything goes, everything is fine – there's no such thing as right and wrong anyway. It's all down to personal choice.' In this individualist behaviour system there are no standards. And so this way of thinking brings about a society that is amoral. We have reached a state generally and personally in which our conscience, the intellect, has become totally dysfunctional. This is why we need meditation. When we meditate, we start to create pure thoughts. Meditation means having a spiritual belief and working with the paradigm that I am not my body, I am a soul.

The power of meditation

Meditation is all about keeping the filter of the intellect so clear and clean that whatever passes through it, only that which is right is allowed to become an action – even words must be passed through this filter, because words have a profound impact on the self as well as on others.

Meditation cleans out the conscience and strengthens it. Meditation makes the conscience so powerful that our actions change and as a result of that our *sanskaras*, or personality traits, change. Meditation has a direct impact on my *sanskaras* too, because when I sit in silence and come to the awareness of my inner being, I resonate with those original *sanskaras* which are truly my own. I come back to that original state of peace, love, purity and happiness. I am no longer looking for these outside myself, and I don't have to search for them anymore. Peace, love, purity and happiness are there within me and I return to them once again.

Meditation is not only the key to changing the vicious cycle of thoughts, actions and *sanskaras*, it transforms them completely. Meditation is not just for five or fifteen minutes, but becomes a state of awareness that I carry throughout the day. This guided meditation will show you how to remain constantly in that higher awareness.

Meditation

Sitting comfortably in silence, I let my body become calm and quiet and I journey inward. When I sit in silence I reinforce my awareness of who I am and I connect with all those inner treasures of peace, love, purity and happiness... they are my own original treasures.

I take this thought with me through the day...

As I walk around, let me walk in the awareness of I, the soul. When I look at others, let me see the soul as my brother, the shining star, and not as strangers of different nationalities, races or religions. Let me connect with the soul who is my brother.

When I eat, let me eat in the awareness that I, the soul, have to care for this vehicle, the body. I know that everything I do can be in the consciousness of materialism – just for the body. Or I can choose to remain in the elevated consciousness and awareness of who I truly am – the soul. That is my choice.

When I face a dilemma or even the simplest choice, I know that I have the ability to choose which state of consciousness I want to be in. I use my intellect to help me choose the right course of action. Am I conscious of just matter or am I conscious of spirit? Am I soul conscious? I let my intellect – my buddhi – make a conscious choice. When my intellect is not conscious, it is asleep. When it is asleep it is only aware of the body. I choose to awaken it... the intellect is the key that will help me unlock the treasures within.

When I need to break free from any vicious habits that have trapped me, I know that my intellect is there to help me. Whether they are habits of anger or ego or attachment, or habits of physical addiction – to the computer, or gossip or drugs, all things that hold me in bondage – this key of my intellect will help me to break free. I meditate to strengthen my conscience and to break free from that circle of habits and attitudes.

When my mind acts like a wild horse, running off in different directions, I know that I can use my intellect and its power of understanding to reign it in. The mind runs out of control because my intellect has no knowledge within it at that time. When the intellect has the understanding that I, the soul, am the creator of my thoughts, I am finally able to take charge of the direction of my mind. When the mind is tamed then the reins are in my hands and I have control... when the reins of my mind are in my control I am able to develop my inner capacity to experience the original qualities that I long for. I know that we long to experience our original qualities because they are our natural state of being. I, the soul, am made up of these qualities... this is why I want to experience them once more.

I come back to these original sanskaras – love, peace, purity, happiness – in silence... meditation keeps my mind on the right track through awareness of who I am... then all those treasures become mine.

Point summary

- Our thoughts lead us to actions. Karma (action) has two dimensions: external and internal; it creates an impact to the external world as well as leaves an imprint on the self.

- Each time I repeat an action, the sanskara, in turn, becomes firmer.

- The intellect acts as a filter which allows only that which is true and right to emerge into action. Meditation cleans out the intellect and strengthens it.

- By increasing the awareness of my true identity as a soul, and getting rid of the illusion of being the body, I am able to discern accurately what is right and wrong, and would only perform actions based on the original qualities of peace, love and wisdom.

Self-reflective question:

How can the self come out of the vicious cycle of negative karma and create beneficial actions which bring about happiness and spiritual upliftment?

Self-experimentation

During the day, keep track of how you use your body, mind and wealth - the three different types of resources we spend energy on - with the understanding that every action produces a consequence.

Anatomy of consciousness

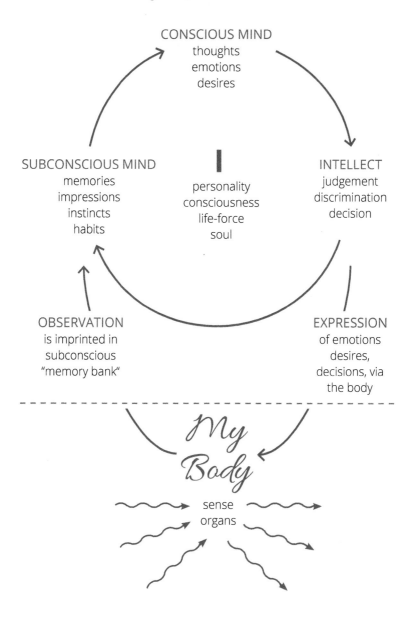

CONSCIOUS MIND
thoughts
emotions
desires

SUBCONSCIOUS MIND
memories
impressions
instincts
habits

personality
consciousness
life-force
soul

INTELLECT
judgement
discrimination
decision

OBSERVATION
is imprinted in
subconscious
"memory bank"

EXPRESSION
of emotions
desires,
decisions, via
the body

My Body

sense
organs

Lesson 5

MASTERING THE SELF

The Hindi word *raja* means 'the king, the sovereign, the master of the self'. The word *yoga* means 'union with the Supreme Soul, or God'. To become the master of the self I need to be able to develop a relationship with my body in which the soul uses my body in the right way, but also cares for my body in the right way, not misusing or abusing it but treating it as an instrument. In Raja Yoga meditation, three simple images are highly effective in bringing us to a state of mastery over the self – and these are a precursor to uniting with the Supreme Soul, which we will look at in the final chapter of the book.

Driving a car

This first image helps us to better understand the relationship of the soul with the body. To practise this technique, simply visualise the soul as a driver and your body as the vehicle. If we think about driving a car, we know that if we get distracted for one moment, an accident may occur. In the same way, if for one moment I, the soul, forget that I am the driver of this vehicle, the body, and I say or do the wrong thing, then there is also danger of an accident happening. This is why as I walk and move through my day I need to practise this awareness. Try saying to yourself at regular intervals through the day, 'I am the driver in charge of this vehicle'. As the driver, you'll need to think about keeping the vehicle well-maintained and fit for the road. Think about this as you plan your menu for the day: are you putting in the right type of fuel for this vehicle – are you even fully aware of the type of fuel that keeps this vehicle functioning at its optimum? Is it keeping all the systems running smoothly or is it perhaps causing problems? Thinking of ourselves as drivers allows us to focus on the relationship of soul and body.

Acting a part

The second useful analogy for understanding that the soul is separate from the body is to imagine the soul as an actor, using the costume of the body to play a part on the stage of the world. The actor is quite separate from the costume. Today, I wear this costume and I play a particular role in the drama, but tomorrow I may not have this costume because I cannot know for how long I will be playing this part. While I have this costume on I, the actor, play my part to the best of my abilities. My roles are all contained within the part I am playing, so at work I take on the role of the manager; that is my role while I am in the office. However, if I go home and behave like a manager, nobody is going to accept it. The manager is my role while I am at work, but at home I have to play the role of a father. Even within that role, I am not simply the authoritative father whose lines include phrases such as, 'You must listen to me!' I also have to play the role of a friend so that my children can connect to me with warmth and playfulness. Even when I am playing the twin roles of father and friend, I have to remain completely flexible, able to adapt to play other roles as they arise. Most of all, I need to remember that while I am playing the role of the father, I am always the soul and it is the soul that is the actor. These roles are my creation. I, the soul, am the actor creating the roles I play but the creator cannot be the creation; therefore I, the soul, cannot be the roles that I am playing.

What happens when we get trapped within a certain role? What happens when we over-identify with our roles, thinking we are only a manager or a father, and these roles become our understanding of who we are? When we do this, we forget our true identity because our sense of self has moved away from the soul and towards the roles we play. When this happens, we lose the knowledge of who we truly are and are no longer able to connect with those inner treasures of peace and love, purity and wisdom that are deep within us. The peaceful soul inside the body plays out different roles. We are not the roles we are playing. They are distinct and separate from the real I. Each of us is an actor playing our roles. I am more than a man or a woman, a son or a daughter, a manager or a father or a friend. To maintain this critical distance, from time to time it is important to step back and observe yourself playing the roles – I guarantee that you will find this completely fascinating and very entertaining! The key to success is to keep in mind the following: when I am performing actions, let me be aware that I am an actor playing my part.

Coming home

The third analogy we use in Raja Yoga to help us come to a state of mastery over the self is to think of the self as a dweller and of the body as a home, temple or other sacred place. When we walk into somebody's home we can gauge the personality of the owner instantly from the state of their home, and whether it is a place of cleanliness or chaos. But quite apart from that external aspect, we also feel the vibrations as we walk into a home. We may feel calm because the atmosphere is welcoming or we may detect a state of tension and wonder what has been taking place before we arrived. Even if the incident happened many hours earlier, the vibrations of conflict or unhappiness linger.

So I need to check this: what are the vibrations like in here, in my body, in my home. I am the dweller and if I am connected with myself then this 'home' will remain in a state of calm and order – which means that it is healthy. When I, the soul, am peaceless and restless and discontented, the impact is evident in the vibrations in my body, my home, and there is disorder. A great deal of research has confirmed that the way in which the mind impacts upon the body and has made connections between a negative state of mind and ill health.

Monitoring awareness

Some people say that they don't have time to meditate, but we all find time to eat and drink. We have to do the cooking and the cleaning; we have to drive to places. These are all part of normal life and all of them offer an opportunity to practise meditation. We can meditate while doing all these other activities very simply – by thinking of one of the three analogies outlined in this chapter. As we do so, we practise awareness of I, the soul, working through our hands. These visualisations allow us to practise this awareness throughout the day: as we walk, eat, drive, clean and cook. Let my hands do the work and my intellect be free. That is the time when I can meditate. When we are vacuuming, for example, we don't think about the vacuum cleaner picking up each particle of dust. We notice this and get on with the job, thinking about all sorts of other things. Rather than thinking about inconsequential matters or dwelling on past concerns or future worries, let me do the job so that I the soul, working through my hands, am cleaning the carpet and also cleaning my soul.

Meditation and life are not separate. Meditation and spirituality are part of life. If I superimpose meditation on every part of life, then meditation becomes part of everything I do. This is self-mastery. When I live in this way, I am the master of the self, master of my thoughts, feelings and personality, but also the master of this body. Then I am using this body in the best possible way to reach my destination of peace, power, happiness and truth. Let us try this out in a practical meditation.

Meditation

Sitting comfortably in silence, I let my body become calm and quiet and I journey inward. I come back to the awareness of I, the inner being of light, the master of this body.

I, the soul, am the master of my eye... I am able to see spirit not body.

I, the soul, am the master of my ear... deciding what is useful information for me to hear and what is likely to pollute me; what I do not need to hear.

I, the soul, am the master of my tongue... I choose what it is I need to share in words... what it is that will be helpful, uplifting, empowering and encouraging... I choose. I decide not to utter words of criticism... words that put others down ... gossip that is petty and irrelevant... I choose.

As I make these choices – choices of seeing, hearing and speaking – and I follow them through, I can feel my own inner power increase. As I become more powerful, I am able to keep my mind on track ... and my mind ... my thoughts ... lead me to my destiny... to discover my inner treasure of peace.
As a master I have the key to all the treasures: peace, love, truth, joy and purity. I remain with this awareness and I come back to the awareness of my physical surroundings... I am aware of my physical surroundings, but still I am the master... connected with my own inner treasures.

Point summary

- To become the master of the self, there needs to be an accurate understanding of the relationship between the body and the soul, in which the soul uses and cares for the body in the right way.

- The three images which bring one to the state of self mastery:

  1 The soul as the driver and the body as the vehicle.

  2 The soul as an actor using the costume of the body on this world stage.

  3 The soul as a dweller and the body as a sacred home.

- Meditation and spirituality are part of life. True self-mastery is when meditation becomes part of everything we do.

- Master of the self is the ruler of my thoughts, feelings, personality and the body, leading them towards the destination of peace, power, happiness and truth.

Self-reflective question:

Why aren't many people able to become the true masters and rulers of the self?

Self-experimentation

Try to perform actions in soul consciousness, that of a detached observer; check when the self is getting too caught up in the pressure of time or in the action itself.

Lesson 6

CONNECTING WITH GOD

As we discovered in the previous chapter, the word *yoga* means 'union, connection and communication with the Supreme'. The more I live with an awareness of the soul, the easier it will be for me to experience yoga – to connect to and communicate with the one who is Supreme, or God. There are, of course, many forms of yoga, but out of all the different methods, traditionally Raja Yoga has been described as being the highest.

In the context of the meditation that we follow, Raja Yoga combines within itself elements of all the other yogas. *Bhakti* yoga is a form of connecting with the Supreme by living a life of devotion and love. *Gyan* yoga is the yoga of knowledge, achieved through self-study and spending time with the yogic scriptures and spiritual teachers. *Buddhi* yoga is the yoga of the intellect, and *Hatha* yoga emphasises the discipline of mind and body required to achieve union with the Supreme. All these different aspects of the yoga are combined within Raja Yoga.

Who is the Supreme?

There is one universal factor that unites every living being on earth – we are all souls. Irrespective of our physical bodies and our lifestyles, we all share the same universal qualities: peace, love, happiness, purity and wisdom. We also share the same spiritual parent. From previous chapters we now understand that the soul is not physical; it is a being of light. So who is God? A simple understanding tells us that God is the Supreme among all souls. Each soul has its goodness, each soul has its own capacity, and out of all souls the Supreme has absolute peace, love, truth, wisdom, purity and joy. There is no mystery and no confusion about this.

The image of God as a point of light acts as a mirror of the soul. It is exactly the same as your own image. A point of light is what you look like, but it is also the image of the Supreme. In appearance there is no difference – no one is bigger and no one is smaller – God has the same form as we do, which is a point of light. Once we accept the concept of the soul and practise awareness of the soul and experience I, the soul, as an inner being of light, then it is easy to connect to the One who is the Supreme Being of Light. The Supreme is the highest in terms of attributes.

What makes us different from God then? All souls come into a human body to play a part on the world stage, but the Supreme is forever beyond birth and death. The Supreme is always constant, too. My qualities can change. One moment I can be loving, but the next moment my love is diluted a little.

One moment there is peace, but the next moment peace has disappeared somewhere. So, although human qualities are always there deep within us, they change and fluctuate in intensity; sometimes they are more and sometimes less, and we go through all our life experiences in that way. The Supreme, however, is forever constant and unchangeable in the full intensity of His qualities.

Meditation and the Supreme

When we meditate, we focus our thoughts on the Supreme and His constant qualities. In Raja Yoga we do not meditate on a holy word or a mantra, on a symbol or an image. You don't need to get into a special posture to meditate or prepare yourself with breathing exercises. All you need to do is to focus your thoughts on the Supreme.

When we have a connection with somebody, what is the basis for the connection? Our thoughts. The words, the telephone calls or the actions will come afterwards. First comes the connection of the mind. So meditation means focusing my thoughts on God. This is very simple because my understanding of God is so simple. God is simply the Supreme Being of Light and the Source of all positive attributes. When I focus my mind on God, I use my thoughts in the way we have been experimenting with and experiencing. That is, I first come into the awareness of the soul, then I detach from my body and come into an awareness of the qualities of my own self. The next step in Raja Yoga meditation is to connect with the Divine, the Supreme Being of Light.

How do we visualise this being? The light is not a physical one, but is instead the light of love, consciousness and truth; a light which gives us a feeling of security and acceptance, of warmth and joy. We need to put aside any images or physical forms that we have associated with God in the past, and instead simply become aware of our own eternal identity. Then we can focus on the Supreme and experience His qualities. Although we may take inspiration from those around us, no human being can actually help us to change, to transform ourselves. We can have a profound realisation or experience and take steps to change, but the power we need to bring about transformation in ourselves comes from God. To know God – to have a connection with God and to draw on His love and power – is the very essence of transformation, and the definition of Raja Yoga meditation.

Transforming ourselves

Transformation is not possible if it is not carried out in the context of truth. God is the One who is Absolute Truth, and so if I stay connected to God, His truth will be able to remove all the falsehood and the illusions I have acquired. He is able to cleanse me and purify me so that I can enter fully into that truth. If I tried to transform myself previously, on my own, it would not have been effective. A great deal of dust has been mixed within the soul and so I could not see the truth, even though it was there in front of me. My connection with God in meditation wipes away that dust so that I become more and more aware of the truth – so aware of it that I am actually able to imbibe truth.

When we find a connection with God, we begin to understand the difference between knowledge and wisdom. Knowledge is just in my head. Although I understand that this is real or that this is truth, that this is right and this is wrong, still I lack the power I need to apply that truth and follow it in my day-to-day life. But when I have both knowledge and a connection with God and am able to draw God's light, love and might into myself, I find that I can follow the right course of action and make it true to my life. Then the practical application of knowledge becomes wisdom. Abstract knowledge on its own is different from the life experience of knowledge based on truth – this is wisdom. When we say somebody is wise it is not simply because they know something; it is because their knowledge has been put into action in their life and so their life experience is full of wisdom.

Like attracts like

In a meditative state, I think about the qualities of the Supreme: the compassion, the love, the power and the purity as well as the truth. Then I can also think about my relationships with God. God as my loving and accepting Mother; God as my Father, who holds my hand and supports and guides me; God as my Teacher, the Ocean of Knowledge; God as my Friend, who is always available and gives me the company of the truth; God as my Beloved, the one I can share intimate feelings with.

In our relationships with God, like attracts like. If, for example, while knowing that God is a Being of Love, we sit in silence with feelings of animosity for another person, then the image of that person will come to mind; it won't be God who comes to our thoughts. If we have feelings of anger, God stays very far away. But if we consciously bring out from within us feelings that are honest, good and positive, then God will come to us. If we come to God with feelings of peace, we can easily approach the Ocean of Peace. So it is important to keep the mind moving in the direction of truth, creating thoughts of the self and thoughts of God. This is meditation.

The purpose of meditation is communication: moving my thoughts towards God so that I connect and I am able to receive from God all His qualities within my own self. Then the dust that I have acquired in my journey through life will all be washed away and my own highest attributes emerge again. I need to practise the consciousness of being detached from the body for a number of reasons. If I am trapped in the awareness of the body, I cannot connect with God and so when I am detached from the body, although I am still in the body, my consciousness no longer settles on people and places and food and situations. My thoughts are focused on God. Detachment from the body allows me to connect with God because the physical body has been the barrier between me and the Supreme. God doesn't have a physical form. Therefore I have to go beyond the consciousness of my physical form to connect with God and experience that subtle state of union. When during the day I practise being a soul and so being detached from the body, I become the master of the body. Then, when I sit in meditation, it is easy for me to experience being away from the body. In Raja Yoga we sometimes use the term 'the bodiless stage', meaning that we are not aware of the body even though the soul is still very much in the body. I can't leave my physical body, but using the power of the mind I can shift my awareness away from the body and instead connect with the Supreme.

Inner power

As a result of meditation, power emerges from within the self – the power of love, peace, purity, truth and happiness. This brings about such incredible inner power that nothing outside can touch you inside. Things may go up and down on the outside, but you will stay true to yourself. You will remain calm and peaceful and you will know what to do, what to say and how to help.

Remaining in this consciousness all day every day offers a wonderful protection from whatever is going on around us – and even from what is going on within our own minds – because for a while after we start to meditate we find that we are still affected by all our memories and the habits we carry within the self: our *sanskaras*, or personality traits.

We need to develop this relationship with God unconsciously and continuously. Then through this relationship, the final state of change, or transformation, will emerge, when the soul returns to its original state, to its highest, natural qualities. Think about this as you follow this guided meditation. Try to keep your body relaxed, but your mind alert.

Meditation

I let the body sit quietly... consciously, I let the body relax... I can feel any tension in the muscles dissolve. I become aware of my own breath. And my breath becomes deeper and calmer... and as my body returns to a state of order and harmony, I focus my attention inside on my own mind.

I look inward... I look at my thoughts... and the speed of my mind slows down. When my thoughts slow down I can be selective and choose only to have the thoughts that I want to have... I choose thoughts of peace and I hold peace in my mind.

In this awareness of peace I begin to see the Being who is the Supreme... a Being of Light... a Being of Truth... a Being of Beauty. I enter the presence of God... I let God's light touch me. God's light is the light of love... a love that is pure, totally accepting and unconditional... I absorb His pure love within my being. I know that I belong to God... and that this is a connection of eternity. This is a relationship that is forever... a love that cleanses... a love that heals... a love that empowers... a love that transforms... a love that guides me. With the power of this love I am able to shed the layers of dust that I had accumulated.

The power of this love awakens my own original truth and beauty. The power of this love connects me with every other soul... this is my eternal family – the whole of humanity. The power of this love reaches out and touches other souls, awakening them. The power of this love touches nature... and nature is healed and restored to a state of harmony. God's love... God's truth... and God's beauty transforms whatever it shines on.

I stay in the awareness of this eternal connection. God's love shines on me... and through me. Keeping my own original qualities of peace, love and truth, which have emerged from within me, and the feeling of the presence of God, I gently bring my thoughts back to the consciousness of my personal surroundings... and I come back with my own qualities shining.

Point summary

- Raja Yoga Meditation is the king of all types of yoga. The combination of bhakti yoga (devoted to the Supreme Soul), buddhi yoga (using the intellect to focus), gyan yoga (based on the divine knowledge) and hatha yoga (discipline of the mind).

- Raja Yoga also means to become the 'king' of one's own mind, the self-sovereign through the power of self-transformation. To have a connection with God and draw on His love and power is the essence of transformation.

- We are all souls, spiritual brothers, who share the same spiritual parent – God.

- God is the Supreme Being of Light and the Source of all positive attributes, with absolute peace, love, truth, wisdom, purity and joy.

- Meditation means concentrating my thoughts on the Divine. When we become aware of our own eternal identity, we can focus on the Supreme Father and experience His qualities.

Self-reflective question:

What is the difference between us, the souls, and God, the Supreme Soul?

Self-experimentation

Experiment with the eternal relationship with God. While sitting in meditation, as well as moving around and performing actions, keep this relationship with you and see what benefits it brings.

When time is short...

Remember these meditation essentials

1 I, the soul, have all the qualities of goodness within me – and each and every one of us also has all these qualities of goodness. Let me remember that.

2 I am the creator of my thoughts, and if I change the quality of my thoughts my whole life begins to change. I must remember this cycle: thoughts lead to actions, which lead to *sanskaras*, or personality traits. That is the key I have to keep the *buddhi*, the intellect, aware. When the intellect is aware, it takes charge of where the mind is going.

3 I must keep connecting with God again and again. I will let God become my Friend so that I can have an ongoing conversation and develop a relationship.

Commonly asked questions

Do we keep our eyes closed or open when we are meditating?

In the form of Raja Yoga we practise, we meditate with our eyes open. This creates a higher awareness as we go about all the things we need to do in life. Practising meditation with the eyes closed might lead to distraction when we open our eyes again. If I keep my eyes open when I meditate and my mind is working on that higher awareness, then I can keep this awareness as I get on with other things in life. When I am alone I can sit looking straight ahead; when I am in a gathering and someone is conducting the meditation I can look towards the centre of their forehead or I can look towards an image of a point of light. Just as I am a non-physical being of light so is the Supreme. So to keep the eyes open is to focus my thoughts on the Supreme.

When is the best time of day for practising meditation?

In Raja Yoga we consider the early morning the best time for daily meditation, and meet for *Amrit Vela* (meditation practice) at 4am each day for 45 minutes. But whether you meditate in the early morning or again at night time, I still ask, 'Well what are you doing all day?' When people say that they have no time for meditation I say whenever you are teaching, looking after children or nursing patients, or whatever your daily task might be – if you are carrying out your work in a meditative state of mind then you are engaging in meditation. Even when we are extremely busy, if we focus on keeping the mind full of awareness and filled with love and faith then in a wonderful way we will be able to see the multi-fold result of meditation. If you are making equal internal spiritual efforts with your thoughts, words and actions you will be recharged all the time and will feel refreshed – you will never feel tired. That is the wonder of meditation.

You mentioned different kinds of yoga. Are all these different yogas connected? Do we progress through them step by step or can we work with Raja Yoga as a beginner?

In my own journey I went straight away to Raja Yoga. When I was growing up my mother used to meditate and so this connected me to meditation and introduced me to Raja Yoga. But many people practise Hatha yoga initially and then come to Raja Yoga or first try other forms of yoga. Every way is fine.

What is the particular relevance of the spot on the forehead between the eyes? Why can't I meditate using another point on the body, such as my navel or by imagining myself out of my body – what is so significant about this point?

The location of the soul within the physical body is just here on the forehead, directly in front of the pineal gland. From this point the soul is able to work though the brain, sending out and receiving information. So the connection between the soul and the body is just here, and from here I can send out thoughts anywhere. When I meditate it is not just a question of focusing my thoughts here at the forehead, but coming to the awareness of who I am – the eternal soul, which is separate from my physical body. This is the location where I do this most easily, but it is only a starting point. Once I have begun my meditation, I become aware of my inner journey and of what is within the soul... and then I am connected with the light of the Supreme. During communal meditation, we communicate best if I look at you with the awareness of soul and then our connection is one of soul to soul, and brother to brother – looking at your navel does not achieve this, but looking at your forehead does!

Can you tell me the difference between meditation, trance and hypnosis? Is there, in fact, a difference?

Yes, there is a big difference between these forms. Meditation is a type of awareness in which I am aware of myself, the eternal being, and I am connected with the Supreme in a very conscious relationship. In comparison there are two types of trance: one pulls me into a different state of consciousness, in which I do not know where I am and who I am connecting with – it could be any spirit anywhere and is very dangerous... so I advise you not to go there. Don't try to have out-of-body experiences to connect with spirits floating around. There is a second type of trance state, in which I am focused on God, and God's love and power pulls me into an altered consciousness. In this altered state I am able to have an understanding of dimensions beyond the physical – so this type of trance is beautiful and positive, but it doesn't happen when or if you ask for it, or even if you work for it. This type of trance arrives as a gift. Other trances in which people aim to become channels and which involve an out-of-body experience are to be avoided completely. So it is best to forget about trance and focus instead on meditation, which will bring you untold benefit.

How do I let go of the past?

As soon as you remember that every moment brings you something new, then it becomes very easy to let go of the past. In my own practice I want to see the transformation happen not only within myself, but I also want to see the changes within my relationships, my interactions, my behaviour – changes in absolutely everything! I want to bring about this power to change so it is very important also to have a feeling of gratitude – and to express thanks to the Supreme Soul. Then I have the awareness that I have this moment and can use it to start over and begin again from now. This is a very interesting way to let go of whatever past you have been holding on to. In this way you will be able to make your awareness completely clean and completely pure whenever you remember the present moment.

Could you explain the nature of truth in more detail, and also tell us more about knowledge and wisdom?

God is the One who is Absolute Truth and as I stay connected with God, God's company is able to remove the falsehoods and illusions that I have acquired and can cleanse and purify me so I can draw towards that truth more and more. I, on my journey through life, have reached a state in which a great deal of dust has become mixed within my soul. Because of this, I can longer discern truth even if it set out in front of me. My connection with God in meditation removes that dust so that I not only become more aware of truth, I become better able to use it practically in my life.

The difference between knowledge and wisdom is this. I might understand what is real and true in my mind, and yet not have the power to follow that truth in my life. This is to have knowledge, but not wisdom. When I have that knowledge and connect with God, drawing light and might and truth within myself, then I am able to apply that knowledge practically in my life – that leads to wisdom. A wise person is anyone who uses knowledge in their life; then he or she has a practical experience of wisdom.

What is the 'bodiless stage' and how by practising this can we connect more and more with the Supreme?

I, the soul, am here in this body. When I leave the body and go away, that is departure. I can practise awareness of being detached from the body, and I need to do this for a number of reasons. If I am trapped in the consciousness of the body then I cannot connect with God. So being detached from the body, but still in it, draws my consciousness away from people, possessions, places, food and situations to increase my focus on God. My body becomes a barrier between me and the Divine because the Supreme doesn't have a physical form. So I have to go beyond the physical form to connect with God and experience a state of union. Throughout the day I need to practice the awareness of being the soul, which is detached from and master of the body. Then when I have a chance to sit in meditation, it will be very easy for me to experience being away from the body. We use the term 'bodiless state' to mean being unaware of the body while being very much within the body. With the power of the mind we can go beyond the body and make contact with God. We use the term 'bodiless stage', but the soul is still very much here, within the forehead.

Is it body-consciousness that has created *sanskaras* (negative personality traits)?

When I am caught up in the consciousness of the body, materialism begins – I associate myself not with the soul, but with the body, ego, anger. Then all negativity begins. Having knowledge of the soul and practising soul-consciousness through meditation is the way to become free of this.

In a family, every person is affected by the actions of other family members. I might be practising meditation myself, but others will still be influenced by the negativity of the everyday world. How can I bring my family, too, back to a state in which I can connect with them and improve their lives?

When you are travelling on a plane and they give safety instructions, one of the things they tell you that when there is an emergency an oxygen mask will fall. The stewards stress how important it is to put on your own oxygen mask before helping anyone else to do so – a child or elderly person, for instance. If you don't secure your own oxygen supply first, you will be unable to help anybody else. The spiritual lesson is the same: look after your own self first. If I don't look after my own self I will never be equipped to look after anyone else. The road we have been travelling has not brought us the happiness we would like, so if I keep going along the same road the pain, suffering and distress will continue. But if I choose to take another branch of the road, by first of all doing something about myself, then there is hope.

I cannot begin with other people, telling them what to do, if I have not addressed my own self. If I am able to change my body-conscious responses to the world – of anger, ego and so on – to responses of peace, pure love and joy, then everyone around me will witness and benefit from my change. The atmosphere of my home will change and then my family will say, 'Mum, what's different? What are you doing?' Even if your family don't state outright that they are benefiting from the new atmosphere you have created, they will be benefiting. Just think how beneficial it is to everyone if the family starts each new day in a home that is peaceful and calm rather than one filled with anger and impatience. So I have to start by transforming myself, and if I am doing the things that I need to, everything else will fall into place.

Would you say that we need to become more introverted in order to meditate?

If we are to look at ourselves deeply, understand our weaknesses and remove them, then yes, we need to become more subtle and introverted, and we also need to take on board how unhelpful extroversion is to the soul. When I am extroverted, my intellect works too much and my focus is on external things. But once I go into a state of introversion I have deep realisations and feel able to cope with everyone I meet and every situation I face. Nowadays many people feel disheartened, while others have the impression that they are moving forwards and are marvellous! But real effort towards self-transformation is incognito and constant. It is not made just for show or to make us happy for only a little while. As we gain greater awareness of the soul through meditation, we naturally become introverted: the mind becomes quiet, the sense organs come under control and the soul realises its true self.

What is the secret of happiness?

Remember that the mind is like a baby; you need to take care of it very well and offer it good food. Treat the mind well and your heart will be happy. Make the quality of your thoughts good and you will be able to watch how your mind and heart become happy. Keep your intellect clear and clean; become honest with yourself. Those who are honest are greatly loved.

What are the aspects of meditation that I should remember above all?

First, try to keep in mind that I, the soul, have great qualities within me and that every person also has these same qualities. Secondly, say to yourself 'I am the creator of my own thoughts and if I change the quality of my thoughts, my whole life will start to change'. It is important to keep the intellect, the *buddhi*, aware so that it takes charge of where the mind is going. Finally, again and again connect with the One above and let God become a friend so that you can have a natural relationship and deepening conversations.

Final thought:

'I, the soul, am peaceful and full of all qualities. I am the creator of my thoughts. The Supreme Being is my friend. Through my thoughts I can come close to the Supreme Being and experience the Supreme as my friend.'

About Sister Jayanti

More than 40 years ago Sister Jayanti dedicated her life to the study, practice and teaching of the ancient system of meditation and spiritual understanding known as Raja Yoga. Since then, she has shared with millions of people worldwide her understanding and experience of the deepest spiritual truths. She is European Director of Brahma Kumaris World Spiritual University (BKWSU).

Sister Jayanti is sought after as a speaker across the globe because she has a unique ability to impart the deepest spiritual truths with the utmost clarity. As well as talking about and teaching meditation, the lecture themes closest to her heart include health, education, racial harmony, women's needs, the religions of the world, peace and international relations. These interests stem from her personal experience: as a young woman from a traditional Asian family growing up in London, she had to face not only the cultural divide but also gender issues. Her deep understanding of spirituality enabled her to understand the role of feminine qualities in personal and world transformation and empowered her to use these in a practical way.

Sister Jayanti places the erosion of spiritual values at the heart of the underlying cause of the crises that the world is facing today, and so she has worked tirelessly to promote positive, human, spiritual values to all sectors of society. In 1980 she was appointed the University's main representative to the United Nations (UN) in Geneva, Switzerland. This has led her to participate in many UN Conferences and projects, in connection with women, development, the environment and youth as well as in a major international project for the United Nations International Year of Peace. As part of this work, she has undertaken extensive research into the role spiritual values play in changing the world.

About the Brahma Kumaris

The Brahma Kumaris is a network of organisations in over 100 countries, with its spiritual headquarters in Mt Abu, India. The University works at all levels of society for positive change. Acknowledging the intrinsic worth and goodness of the inner self, the University teaches a practical method of meditation that helps people to cultivate their inner strengths and values.

The University also offers courses and seminars on such topics as positive thinking, overcoming anger, stress relief and self-esteem, encouraging spirituality in daily life. This spiritual approach is also brought into healthcare, social work, education, prisons and other community settings.

The University's Academy in Mount Abu, Rajasthan, India, offers individuals from all backgrounds a variety of life-long learning opportunities to help them recognise their inherent qualities and abilities in order to make the most of their lives.

All courses and activities are offered free of charge.

Visit www.brahmakumaris.org for more information.
For Publications visit www.inspiredstillness.com

How and where to find out more

SPIRITUAL HEADQUARTERS
PO Box No 2, Mount Abu 307501, Rajasthan, India
Tel: (+91) 2974-238261 to 68
Fax: (+91) 2974-238883
E-mail: abu@bkivv.org

INTERNATIONAL CO-ORDINATING OFFICE & REGIONAL OFFICE FOR EUROPE AND THE MIDDLE EAST

Global Co-operation House, 65-69 Pound Lane,
London, NW10 2HH, UK
Tel: (+44) 20-8727-3350
Fax: (+44) 20-8727-3351
E-mail: london@brahmakumaris.org

REGIONAL OFFICES

AFRICA
Global Museum for a Better World, Maua Close,
off Parklands Road, Westlands
PO Box 123, Sarit Centre, Nairobi, Kenya
Tel: (+254) 20-374-3572
Fax: (+254) 20-374-3885
E-mail: nairobi@brahmakumaris.org

THE AMERICAS AND THE CARIBBEAN

Global Harmony House, 46 S. Middle Neck Road,
Great Neck, NY 11021, USA
Tel: (+1) 516-773-0971
Fax: (+1) 516-773-0976
E-mail: newyork@brahmakumaris.org

AUSTRALIA AND SOUTH EAST ASIA

181 First Ave, Five Dock, Sydney, NSW 2046, Australia
Tel: (+61) 2-9716-7066
Fax: (+61) 2-9716-7795
E-mail: fivedock@au.brahmakumaris.org

RUSSIA , CIS AND THE BALTIC COUNTRIES

Brahma Kumaris World Spiritual University
2, Lobachika, Bldg. No. 2
Moscow – 107140
RUSSIA
Tel: (+7) : +7499 2646276
Fax: (+7) 495-261-3224
E www: brahmakumarisru.com
 www: spiritual-development.ru
E-mail: moscow@brahmakumaris.org